Chapter by Chapter Bible Study

Malachi

CHAPTER BY CHAPTER
BIBLE STUDY
Malachi

An Easy-to-Use Study of
an Entire Book of the Bible

Troy Schmidt

Chapter by Chapter Bible Study: An Easy-to-Use Study of an Entire Book of the Bible—Malachi (VOLUME 4)

Copyright @ 2022 by Troy Schmidt
All rights reserved
First edition
Printed September, 2022

Printed in the United States of America

Cover design / typesetting by David Hicks

For more information about the Author, go to
www.troyeschmidt.com

Scriptures taken from the Holy Bible, New International Version®, NIV®. Copyright © 1973, 1978, 1984, 2011 by Biblica, Inc.™ Used by permission of Zondervan. All rights reserved worldwide.www.zondervan.com The "NIV" and "New International Version" are trademarks registered in the United States Patent and Trademark Office by Biblica, Inc.™

ISBN: 9798353434771

Chapter by Chapter Bible Study

There are 66 books in the Bible. Some of them long, covering massive amounts of history. Some of them short and we wonder why they are there.

Christians believe every single word in the Bible is there for a reason, inspired by God. That means every book, every chapter, every word has a purpose.

Many studies are rich in details, drilling down deep into God's word. A small group can spend ten, twelve, fifteen weeks consuming thought-provoking wisdom every time they meet. That's a good thing, but these studies are different.

Inspired by CHAPTER BY CHAPTER: AN EASY-TO-USE SUMMARY OF THE ENTIRE BIBLE (Amazon), *Chapter By Chapter Bible Studies* tackle one book at a time, one chapter at a time, giving relevant attention to their history, meaning and application. It's everything you need to teach a thorough, complete and thought-provoking study, but at a slightly quicker pace.

Chapter By Chapter Bible Studies are formatted so easily they can be picked up at the last minute and taught comprehensively. Each study walks you through a chapter using a number of teaching tools:

- FACTS (context and background information)
- QUESTIONS (answers to difficult passages)
- DISCUSS (informative and fun interaction)
- FAITH (inspiring thoughts to motivate you)
- READ (a significant passage worth hearing)

But there's more to a bible study than just one meeting. Each *Chapter by Chapter Bible Study* provides a daily prayer guide for the teacher to use leading up to the study and for the student to use when the small group finishes, making sure the impact of the book continues for days to come. A Prayer Journal records prayer requests as a reference point to remember how God is working in lives of your people. There's even a fun quiz to test the class and see how well they paid attention.

Each *Chapter by Chapter Bible Study* inspires conversation, insight and application for the experienced and first time teacher to get the most out of each chapter of the greatest book ever written.

MALACHI QUICK FACTS

Number of Chapters: *4*
The Author: *Malachi*
Approximately written: *450-430 BC (To the Jews living in Judah after the exile to Babylon)*

FACT: This is the last book of the Old Testament, the 12ᵗʰ of 12 books in a section called The Minor Prophets. These books are not minor because of significance. They simply contain less words (from one to fourteen chapters) unlike the Major Prophets such as Isaiah, Jeremiah and Ezekiel with fifty to sixty chapters.

FACT: Malachi marks the last time God spoke through a prophet until John the Baptist showed up over 400 years later in the New Testament.

FACT: "Malachi" was the name of the prophet who spoke this message. His name comes from the Hebrew word "My messenger." Malachi was God's messenger to those living in Judah (the region) and Jerusalem (the city) after the Jews returned to the area following their 70-year exile in Babylon.

FACT: Was God mad, which explains his silence for so long after Malachi? Or did he have nothing nice to say so he said nothing at all? No. He had a plan. He communicated that plan. Now it will take 400 years for that plan to fall into place.

FAITH: God has some hard things to say to his people, but he always gives hope. Receive the good as encouragement and the bad as learning.

DISCUSS: **Would you trust God if he took 400 years to answer you?**

QUESTION: What is the book of Malachi about?

Malachi was written 400 years before Jesus was born. It was the last time God spoke to a prophet in Israel until John the Baptist announced the Messiah's coming. Malachi pointed out the spiritual discrepancies in the rebuilt Israel. The people had returned one hundred plus years before Malachi from exile in Persia/Babylon. The Israelites did not understand that they were repeating all the sins that got them exiled in the first place.

- The offerings were defiled. The sacrifices weren't the best, but the worst of the flock.
- The priests weren't doing their job.
- The people were marrying foreign women and bringing foreign gods into the nation.
- They weren't showing justice.

Despite their disobedience, God showed mercy and promised to love them. He also promised to send a messenger—Elijah—to refine them and guide them. That messenger arrived 400 years later. His name was John the Baptist and he prepared the way for Jesus Christ whom he baptized.

MALACHI 1

QUICK SUMMARY

The Lord said to the prophet Malachi that he loved Jacob but hated Esau. God crushed Edom and reduced it to ruins. God then spoke against the priests who offered lame and diseased sacrifices to him. Shut the temple doors! God is a great king to be feared by the nations! You can't treat him this way.

FACT: **Malachi 1:2** – Malachi proposes questions that the people were probably asking, such as "How have you loved us?" or "How have we shown contempt for your name?" The questions reveal Israel's arrogance and ignorance. "Who, us? What have we done?" There are three questions in this chapter (verses 2, 6, 7)

FACT: **Malachi 1:2-3** – How can God hate? God was talking about Israel and Edom (the countries) not necessarily Isaac and Esau (the people) who birthed these nations. God blessed both Esau and Isaac with many sons. Later on, Esau's nation of Edom always looked for ways to destroy Israel and that kind of ticked God off. God loves unconditionally but there's a point when he must punish. His purpose for the punishment is for the punished to repent and return to God.

FACT: **Malachi 1:4**– Edom was arrogant, thinking they could rebuild. God said that wasn't possible. They will be demolished.

DISCUSS: **Have you seen God's greatness with your own eyes? (1:5)**

FACT: **Malachi 1:6-8** – Instead of offering the best animal from their flock, the people offered the blind, damaged and injured ones – the ones they didn't want anyway. The priests accepted it. It would be like your parents giving you a broken, rusty bike with flat tires and saying, "Happy birthday!" What would you think?

FACT: Malachi 1:6– While Malachi stated questions the people may be asking, God communicated his own questions, such as "Where is the respect I deserve?" and "Would the governor be okay with the treatment you show me?"

DISCUSS: Do you think God is pleased with your offerings? (1:9)

READ: *"Oh, that one of you would shut the temple doors, so that you would not light useless fires on my altar! I am not pleased with you," says the LORD Almighty, "and I will accept no offering from your hands. Malachi 1:10*

FACT: Malachi 1:10– God wanted the temple doors shut to keep the unauthorized out. Only priests called by his name could be inside the temple working. The temple had become overrun with outsiders doing whatever they wanted and in the process they defiled it.

DISCUSS: Would you eat an injured, lame or diseased animal? (1:13)

FAITH: Malachi 1:13– How can our offerings be lame or damaged? Maybe we don't give God enough. Is your attitude at the offering time contemptuous or grateful? A sour attitude spoils the offering.

FAITH: Malachi 1:14 – Are you giving your best to God or the leftovers? Do you pray and multi-task by checking your emails and texts? Do you read the Bible and watch Instagram at the same time? Do you serve God in order to get community service hours? He should get all of our heart and our attention.

MALACHI 2

QUICK SUMMARY

God promised to send a curse to the priests for dishonoring his name. God established this covenant with them because Levi revered God and spoke truth, walking in peace and uprightness. A priest's lips should preserve knowledge, but since they have turned away, God humiliated them. Judah had been unfaithful, marrying foreign women. The people flood the altar with tears yet were unfaithful to their wives. God hates divorce. The people weary God with their words.

FACT: **Malachi 2:3** – Did God just say he would smear the priests' faces with animal doo-doo? Yes. He's pretty mad at them. They caused many to stumble in their faith and they were unfaithful to their wives.

FACT: **Malachi 2:4-6** – Levi was a son of Jacob (Israel). Levi had three sons: Gershon, Kohath and Merari.. In the time of Moses, those descendants were responsible to carry the tabernacle through the wilderness and set it up. Moses and his brother Aaron were Levites also. Through Aaron came the priestly line. God made covenants with the Levites back to the time of Exodus and Leviticus and now these priests were not following those rules.

FAITH: **Malachi 2:8** – If you are in a position of leadership in the church, God holds you to a higher standard. The priests of Malachi's day did more to draw people away from God rather than draw people to God.

DISCUSS: Why is a "dangerous" woman attractive to a man? (2:11)

FAITH: **Malachi 2:13-14** – People cry and complain to God wondering why these terrible things are happening to them. The answer is…*they* are the problem. People don't like to blame themselves so they are quick to blame God.

DISCUSS: **Have you seen any unfaithful relationships restored? (2:14)**

DISCUSS: **Who are the only people who like divorce? (2:16)**

READ: *"The man who hates and divorces his wife," says the LORD, the God of Israel, "does violence to the one he should protect," says the LORD Almighty.*

So be on your guard, and do not be unfaithful. Malachi 2:16

FAITH: **Malachi 2:16** – God compared the people's separation from him to a divorce. A divorce breaks a marriage promise. God does not break promises. He called a broken promise "violence" to another. It's like tearing one's arm from one's body or curb-stomping someone's soul.

QUESTION: **Does God hate divorce? (2:14-16)**

God hates divorce because divorce is about breaking a promise. God never breaks a promise. It's a value to him. Promise breaking is foreign to God and detestable. Two people become one through marriage and splitting them up tears them apart. We think, "I'll learn to live without the other person." True, but there are scars and daily pain. You'll never be the same. God wants a man and a woman to get married and be fruitful and multiply. Divorce destroys that purpose. God hates when his people hurt and suffer.

MALACHI 3

QUICK SUMMARY

   God promised to send a messenger, who, like a refiner's fire or a launderer's soap, would refine and purify the people. The people who defrauded, practiced sorcery, adulterers and perjurers would be put on trial. God asked everyone to return to him. The people want to know what they did wrong. God replied that they stole from his tithes and offerings. God told them to test him to see if they brought the whole tithe to him and see whether God would bless them. God said he would remember the righteous.

READ: *"I will send my messenger, who will prepare the way before me. Then suddenly the Lord you are seeking will come to his temple; the messenger of the covenant, whom you desire, will come," says the LORD Almighty. Malachi 3:1*

FACT: **Malachi 3:1** – John the Baptist was that messenger. Jesus quoted this verse in Matthew 11:10 to confirm that.

FAITH: **Malachi 3:2-4** – Both a refiner's fire and a launderer's soap purify and clean. God wants us cleansed by any means of our sins—water or fire.

FACT: **Malachi 3:6** – God does not change. What a relief. We can count on the same God from 2,000 to 4,000 years ago to be the same always.

DISCUSS: **Have you ever been robbed? (3:8)**

READ: *"Will a mere mortal rob God? Yet you rob me. "But you ask, 'How are we robbing you?'*

7

"In tithes and offerings. You are under a curse—your whole nation—because you are robbing me. Bring the whole tithe into the storehouse, that there may be food in my house. Test me in this," says the LORD Almighty, "and see if I will not throw open the floodgates of heaven and pour out so much blessing that there will not be room enough to store it. Malachi 3:8-10

QUESTION: How should I tithe? (2:7-8, 12-13; 3:8-10)

The prophet Malachi addressed some issues with the people in Israel when it came to tithing. The word "tithe" means "ten percent." First of all, they did not put their heart into the tithe. It wasn't a gift to God but their way of getting rid of the broken, discarded animals (2:7-8). It's like paying your taxes with yard sale items. Even the government would not accept it. Shouldn't we give God our best? Shouldn't we give our whole tithe?

Second, they robbed God by not giving him enough, falling short of the value he is owed (2:12-13). They robbed the ability to minister to people and show them the love of God. They defiled the whole process of loving God through their improper tithing. It would be like giving your wife dead roses. If you love, you give your best.

Tithing is an expression of trust and it has rewards. God told them to "test" him and see if God would bless them—by giving what they were supposed to give (ten percent), in the way they were supposed to give it (their first and their best). Tithing can bring blessing (3:8-10). So, give the whole tithe and watch what God can do.

FAITH: Malachi 3:7,9,13,14 – Again, God quotes what he knows the people were thinking when he accused them of wrongdoing. "How are we to return?" (7) "How are we robbing you?" (9) "What have we said against you?" (13) "It is futile to serve God." (14) God knows every excuse and resistance on our hearts. He's heard them for thousands of years and they haven't changed much over time.

DISCUSS: **Have you ever tested God with your offerings? (3:10)**

FAITH: **Malachi 3:10** – God never says to test him in the Bible except this one time and that's by giving our full tithe and seeing whether God blesses them or not. If we are faithful with our giving, God said he will be faithful in his blessing. This is a promise. Test God and give faithfully and see if he doesn't "throw open the floodgates" in response.

FAITH: **Malachi 3:11-12** – God's blessing isn't only what he gives but what he prevents. He prevents invasion, pests, famine, sometimes things that we know and others we don't.

FAITH: **Malachi 3:16-18** – God looks for faithful people to bless. Many times it's just a small group of followers who hold out until the end. The difference between the righteous and the wicked he wants to communicate to the world is that those who serve God are blessed.

MALACHI 4

QUICK SUMMARY

The day was coming when the arrogant and evildoer would be reduced to stubble and the righteous will rise and frolic. Remember the laws of Moses. God would send the prophet Elijah before the great and dreadful day of the Lord comes. He would turn the hearts of parents to children and children to their parents or strike the land with total destruction.

DISCUSS: **Have you ever gone outside and frolicked like a well-fed calf? (4:2)**

READ: *"See, I will send the prophet Elijah to you before that great and dreadful day of the LORD comes. He will turn the hearts of the parents to their children, and the hearts of the children to their parents; or else I will come and strike the land with total destruction." Malachi 4:5-6*

FACT: **Malachi 4:5** – Jesus confirmed in Matthew 11:10 that this "Elijah" was John the Baptist.

DISCUSS: **What would it look like if our parents' hearts turned to the children? (4:6)**

FAITH: **Malachi 4:6** – John the Baptist turned the hearts of the parents to begin them thinking about the faith of next generation. People began to get serious about their faith with the coming of the Messiah. Today, since Jesus promised to return one day, we should be getting ready and preparing others in our family too. Having faith isn't just saving yourself, but making sure future generations find Jesus.

FACT: **Malachi 4:5-6** – The last words of the Old Testament told the people to look for a prophet. For the next 400 years no prophet spoke to the people. Still, the people waited. When John the Baptist baptized in the wilderness, the religious leaders asked him in John 1:21, "Are you Elijah?" These words in Malachi resonated with the people. They were watching.

QUESTION: **Who was the messenger or Elijah prophesied in Malachi? (3:1-4, 4:5-6)**

The "Elijah" Malachi promised turned out to be John the Baptist who arrived 400 years later after the writings of Malachi. John the Baptist was Jesus' cousin and prepared the people's hearts for the great coming the Lord. Little did everyone suspect that it would literally be God in human flesh, coming in the form of Jesus. And it was Jesus who confirmed John the Baptist's "Elijah" identity, quoting Malachi.

As John's disciples were leaving, Jesus began to speak to the crowd about John: "What did you go out into the wilderness to see? A reed swayed by the wind? If not, what did you go out to see? A man dressed in fine clothes? No, those who wear fine clothes are in kings' palaces. Then what did you go out to see? A prophet? Yes, I tell you, and more than a prophet. This is the one about whom it is written:

"'I will send my messenger ahead of you,
who will prepare your way before you.'

Truly I tell you, among those born of women there has not risen anyone greater than John the Baptist; yet whoever is least in the kingdom of heaven is greater than he. From the days of John the Baptist until now, the kingdom of heaven has been subjected to violence, and violent people have been raiding it. For all the Prophets and the Law prophesied until John. And if you are willing to accept it, he is the Elijah who was to come. Whoever has ears, let them hear. Matthew 11:7-15

John the Baptist was a type of Elijah, a prophet, a proclaimer of truth, though not a miracle worker like Elijah was.

11

John was not literally Elijah, who later showed up on the Mount of Transfiguration next to Jesus and Moses.

Jesus replied, "To be sure, Elijah comes and will restore all things. But I tell you, Elijah has already come, and they did not recognize him, but have done to him everything they wished. In the same way the Son of Man is going to suffer at their hands." Then the disciples understood that he was talking to them about John the Baptist. Matthew 17:11-13

God's final words in the Old Testament were to prepare people for Jesus' coming and John the Baptist's preaching in the wilderness would be the next great sign that God was coming soon.

His job was to announce that someone even greater than him was coming—the son of God himself, Jesus Christ. That would begin a new chapter, a new covenant, for the world.

QUESTION: What happened in the world between the time of Malachi and Matthew?

A lot happened in those 400 years. God needed to set up the world for Jesus to return. During the time of Malachi, the Persians were in power. The transition of world power then shifted to the Greeks, then to the Romans.

- The Greeks led by Alexander the Great conquered Israel in 333/331 BC. The Greeks brought a common language (Greek/Aramaic) to the region so that later the disciples could witness to many people in one language.
- The Maccabees (Jewish revolutionaries) revolted against Greece between 167-160 BC. Religious leaders and Pharisees rose in power.
- Rome became an empire winning the Battle of Corinth in 146 BC (taking Greece), then beating Cleopatra and Mark Antony in Alexandria in 30 BC (taking Egypt). Roman general Pompey defeated Jerusalem in 63 BC.
- With Rome in power, there came peace throughout the region. Rome took a strong upper hand against crime, even crucifying people out in the open. God sent out the disciples during a time of safety to explain a message of peace to the world.
- Rome created many roads so the Gospel could spread.
- The crucifixion death sentence needed to be perfected by the Romans. Its brutality showed the extent of God's love to send his son to die for us.
- The religious leaders of Israel became corrupt and full of pride that they would want someone like Jesus killed. God created an enemy to fulfill his purposes.

As you can see, God was working over those 400 years to unleash Christianity into the world.

FINAL POINTS

1. God gets the last word.

God's last words in the Old Testament are hopeful, but not flattering. He sees our sin and has no problem pointing it out and sending people to call it out. We love all the benefits of faith, God's love for us and Jesus' sacrifice for us, and yet we shrug off the condemnation and punishment of God towards sin, thinking that's for the unbelievers, not me. Let God get the last word – he loves you but doesn't want to leave you the way you are.

2. God is working when you don't think he's working.

Four hundred years of silence is painful. God was not pulling a silent treatment on the people, merely saying "Dwell on the words of Malachi and I'll speak when everything's ready." For four simple chapters, God said be obedient, pay your tithes, don't break promises, get ready for the next prophet and the day when he arrives on earth. That "day of the Lord" would change everything. God was getting everything in place for Jesus. That's true in your life too when God's silent and nothing seems to be happening.

3. Don't rob God.

One of the main indicators of people's lack of faith is their giving. When their giving of tithes and offering slack off or get sloppy, you will see other areas of their life slipping away. Giving is an expression of faith and trust in God. My offering says, "I love you, Lord." When we fail to give, we are stealing from the funds which can be used to further God's kingdom. God sees that as robbery.

14

4. The day of the Lord is coming.

The "day of the Lord" in Old Testament language was an expression meaning "a day of judgment" and/or "a day when God will show up and make things right." For prophets like Isaiah, Ezekiel and Jeremiah, that "day" was God allowing the enemies of God's people to take away their nation. God didn't show up physically, but nations like Assyria and Babylon were his tools and expressions of judgment.

In the Gospels, Jesus represented the "day of the Lord" by literally and physically showing up to judge the people for their failures and giving them an ultimate, final solution for sin.

It didn't all narrow down to a single, 24-hour day, but thirty-three years while Jesus existed on this planet, building up his three-year ministry and then that three-day game changer of death and resurrection. Many days filled that "day of the Lord."

Another "day of the Lord" is coming and this one is final. Jesus will return after 2,000 years of silence and get the last word. He's definitely working and speaking. We don't need any more information or revelation. We have everything we need to know.

Get ready and get others ready...Jesus is coming any day and after that, there's no second chance.

QUICK QUIZ QUESTIONS

Q: How did God believe the people showed contempt for God?

A: _____ (Malachi 1:6-7)

Q: What kind of animal sacrifices were the priests offering to God?

A: _____ (Malachi 1:13)

Q: Whose teachings caused many to stumble?

A: _____ (Malachi 2:8)

Q: God said Judah has been unfaithful to God as a man is unfaithful to who?

A: _____ (Malachi 2:14)

Q: Who was the "messenger" that Malachi prophesied about and Jesus confirmed?

A: _____ (Malachi 3:1, Matthew 11:10)

Q: Malachi compared God's ability to cleanse to what two jobs that use fire and soap?

A: _____ (Malachi 3:2)

Q: How were the people robbing God?

A: _____ (Malachi 3:8)

TOUGH QUESTIONS ABOUT MALACHI

Important themes:

- The people offered sick, injured and blind animals for sacrifices. Don't give the leftovers to God. Give him your best. (Malachi 1:8)
- God's leaders must be examples for the people in order to lead them to God. (Malachi 2:1-2)
- Malachi prophesied a "messenger" also known as Elijah who would come one day. Four hundred years later, that was John the Baptist. (Malachi 3:1, 4:5)
- People rob God by not giving him the correct tithes and offerings. (Malachi 3:8)
- God asked to be tested (the only time in scripture) by giving him tithes and seeing if he doesn't bless the giver in return (Malachi 3:10-11)

What is the book of Malachi about?

Malachi was written 400 years before Jesus was born. It was the last time God spoke to a prophet in Israel until John the Baptist announced the Messiah's coming. Malachi pointed out the spiritual discrepancies in the rebuilt Israel. The people had returned one hundred plus years before Malachi from exile in Persia/Babylon. The Israelites did not understand that they were repeating all the sins that got them exiled in the first place.

- The offerings were defiled. The sacrifices weren't the best, but the worst of the flock.
- The priests weren't doing their job.
- The people were marrying foreign women and bringing foreign gods into the nation.
- They weren't showing justice.

Despite their disobedience, God showed mercy and promised to love them. He also promised to send a messenger—Elijah—to refine them and guide them. That messenger arrived

400 years later. His name was John the Baptist and he prepared the way for Jesus Christ who he baptized.

Malachi 2:7-8, 12-13; 3:8-10

How should I tithe?

The prophet Malachi addressed some issues with the people in Israel when it came to tithing. The word "tithe" means "ten percent." First of all, they did not put their heart into the tithe. It wasn't a gift to God but their way of getting rid of the broken, discarded animals (2:7-8). It's like paying your taxes with yard sale items. Even the government would not accept it. Shouldn't we give God our best? Shouldn't we give our whole tithe?

Second, they robbed God by not giving him enough, falling short of the value he is owed (2:12-13). They robbed the ability to minister to people and show them the love of God. They defiled the whole process of loving God through their improper tithing. It would be like giving your wife dead roses. If you love, you give your best.

Tithing is an expression of trust and it has rewards. God told them to "test" him and see if God would bless them—by giving what they were supposed to give (ten percent), in the way they were supposed to give it (their first and their best). Tithing can bring blessing (3:8-10). So, give the whole tithe and watch what God can do.

Malachi 2:14-16

Does God hate divorce?

God hates divorce because divorce is about breaking a promise. God never breaks a promise. It's a value to him. Promise breaking is foreign to God and detestable. Two people become one through marriage and splitting them up tears them apart. We think, "I'll learn to live without the other person." True, but there are scars and daily pain. You'll never be the same. God wants a man and a woman to get married and be fruitful and multiply. Divorce destroys that purpose. God hates when his people hurt and suffer.

Malachi 3:1-4, 4:5-6

Who was the messenger or Elijah prophesied in Malachi?

The "Elijah" Malachi promised turned out to be John the Baptist who arrived 400 years later from the writing of the book. John the Baptist was Jesus' cousin and prepared the people's hearts for the great coming the Lord. Little did everyone suspect that it would literally be God in human flesh, coming in the form of Jesus. And it was Jesus who confirmed John the Baptist's "Elijah" identity, quoting Malachi.

As John's disciples were leaving, Jesus began to speak to the crowd about John: "What did you go out into the wilderness to see? A reed swayed by the wind? If not, what did you go out to see? A man dressed in fine clothes? No, those who wear fine clothes are in kings' palaces. Then what did you go out to see? A prophet? Yes, I tell you, and more than a prophet. This is the one about whom it is written:

"'I will send my messenger ahead of you,
  who will prepare your way before you.'

Truly I tell you, among those born of women there has not risen anyone greater than John the Baptist; yet whoever is least in the kingdom of heaven is greater than he. From the days of John the Baptist until now, the kingdom of heaven has been subjected to violence, and violent people have been raiding it. For all the Prophets and the Law prophesied until John. And if you are willing to accept it, he is the Elijah who was to come. Whoever has ears, let them hear. Matthew 11:7-15

John the Baptist was a type of Elijah, a prophet, a proclaimer of truth, though not a miracle worker like Elijah was. John was not literally Elijah, who later showed up on the Mount of Transfiguration next to Jesus and Moses.

Jesus replied, "To be sure, Elijah comes and will restore all things. But I tell you, Elijah has already come, and they did not recognize him, but have done to him everything they wished. In the same way the Son of Man is going to suffer at their hands." Then

19

the disciples understood that he was talking to them about John the Baptist. Matthew 17:11-13

God's final words in the Old Testament were to prepare people for Jesus' coming and John the Baptist's preaching in the wilderness would be the next great sign that God was coming soon.

Time to Pray Through Malachi

MALACHI 1

READ: MALACHI 1

Scripture focus:	*When you offer blind animals for sacrifice, is that not wrong? When you sacrifice lame or diseased animals, is that not wrong? Try offering them to your governor! Would he be pleased with you? Would he accept you?" says the LORD Almighty.* (1:8)
Time:	Around 430 BC
People:	Priests, Israelites
Place:	Israel
What's Happening:	God did not like the sacrifices the people offered to Him – blind, injured and damaged animals. He said the people profaned His temple.

PRAYER

Dear God,
You choose to love who You want to love and hate who You want to hate. That's Your prerogative. But as my Father, I choose to love You. And if You are my Father and my master, then I should show You respect by giving You my best. If I give You anything that's stolen, broken, outdated, worn out, expired, I'm saying that's all Your worth. I wouldn't give that to my neighbor or friend, so why would it be accept to dump it on You? I should give You whatever is the best, purest, heathiest and optimal. You deserve the best because You've given me the best.

KEEP PRAYING...
"I have defiled You by giving You..."
"I need to give more to..."
"You've given me the best by..."

I FEEL GOD IS SAYING TO ME...

_____
_____
_____
_____

MALACHI 2

READ: MALACHI 2

Scripture focus: *You ask, "Why?" It is because the LORD is the witness between you and the wife of your youth. You have been unfaithful to her, though she is your partner, the wife of your marriage covenant.* (2:14)

Time: Around 430 BC

People: Priests, Israelites

Place: Israel, Judah

What's Happening: God was not happy with the way the priests handled the sacrifices nor the way people broke their promises to Him, like a divorce.

PRAYER

Dear God,

I pray for Christian leaders. They are held to a higher standard if they stand and profess their love for You then go out and do differently. They will not be blessed, but cursed. You make a covenant with us that is about life and peace. We need to be reverent about that truth and not turn people away from it. We must preserve knowledge and keep our covenant with You. Our actions are like an unfaithful spouse seeking out other partners. It's our fault. We cry and weep and blame when we don't get our way, but we're to blame. We've left You to the point of completely severing the relationship like a divorce. We can't let that happen. We must be faithful and be on guard nothing comes between us.

KEEP PRAYING...

"I am guilty for causing others to stumble by…"

"I broke the covenant with You by…"

"I can't blame You any longer. It's my fault that…"

I FEEL GOD IS SAYING TO ME...

_____

_____

_____

_____

MALACHI 3

READ: MALACHI 3

Scripture focus: *Bring the whole tithe into the storehouse, that there may be food in my house. Test me in this," says the LORD Almighty, "and see if I will not throw open the floodgates of heaven and pour out so much blessing that there will not be room enough to store it.* (3:10)

Time: Around 430 BC

People: The messenger, the Israelites

Place: Israel

What's Happening: God told the people to stop robbing Him of tithes but to test Him to see if He doesn't provide.

PRAYER

Dear God,

You always find a messenger to speak to us. In this case it was John the Baptist proclaiming the coming of Jesus Christ. What a message that was! A message of purity and cleansing, from sins. You do not change. You've always hated sin and always provide a way for us to return to You. However, in response, we rob You and take advantage of Your grace. We trust more in money than for You to provide. So You ask us to test and see if You don't provide when we give our tithes. Thank you for sparing me despite my disobedience. Thank you for showing me compassion as a father shows his child.

KEEP PRAYING...

"When it comes to giving my tithe..."

"I trust more in..."

"Refine me and purify me of..."

I FEEL GOD IS SAYING TO ME...

_____
_____
_____
_____

MALACHI 4

READ: MALACHI 4

Scripture focus: *"See, I will send the prophet Elijah to you before that great and dreadful day of the LORD comes. He will turn the hearts of the parents to their children, and the hearts of the children to their parents; or else I will come and strike the land with total destruction."* (4:5-6)

Time: Around 430 BC

People: The Israelites, Elijah

Place: Israel

What's Happening: God foretold of an "Elijah" that was coming, confirmed by Jesus as John the Baptist. This final prophecy was the last word in the Old Testament for 400 years.

PRAYER

Dear God,
You have an emergency escape plan. There's a day coming, I know, where no one will escape judgement. This earth and all I know will go up in flames. No roots or branches will be left, giving any possibility of future growth. But if I revere Your name, You will rise up in my life with a glimmer of daylight, hope for the future. I will frolic with joy and walk over evil as I keep Your law. Yes, that plan will take time, like Your plan to bring John the Baptist/Elijah to this earth. But I can wait, while You turn hearts to You, our eternal, gracious and loving Father.

KEEP PRAYING...

"Your escape plan gives me a way out of..."
"Your plans take time and I'm impatient..."
"Turn my heart away from _____ and more to You..."

I FEEL GOD IS SAYING TO ME...

_____
_____
_____
_____

WHAT I LEARNED FROM MALACHI

_____

_____

_____

_____

_____

_____

_____

_____

_____

_____

_____

_____

_____

_____

_____

_____

QUICK QUIZ ANSWERS

Q: How did God believe the people showed contempt for God?
A: **By defiled food offerings** (Malachi 1:6-7)

Q: What kind of animal sacrifices were the priests offering to God?
A: **Blind, injured and lame** (Malachi 1:13)

Q: Whose teachings caused many to stumble?
A: **The priests** (Malachi 2:8)

Q: God said Judah has been unfaithful to God as a man is unfaithful to who?
A: **His wife** (Malachi 2:14)

Q: Who was the "messenger" that Malachi prophesied about and Jesus confirmed?
A:**John the Baptist** (Malachi 3:1/Matthew 11:10)

Q: Malachi compared God's ability to cleanse to what two jobs that use fire and soap?
A: **A refiner and a launderer** (Malachi 3:2)

Q: How were the people robbing God?
A: **In their tithes and offerings** (Malachi 3:8)

PRAYER JOURNAL

GOD DESERVES ALL THE PRAISE FOR

_____

_____

_____

_____

_____

_____

_____

_____

_____

_____

_____

_____

_____

_____

_____

_____

_____

_____

FAMILY/FRIENDS/NEIGHBORS I AM PRAYING FOR

_____

_____

_____

_____

_____

_____

_____

_____

_____

_____

_____

_____

_____

_____

_____

_____

_____

_____

_____

SALVATIONS I AM PRAYING FOR

_____

_____

_____

_____

_____

_____

_____

_____

_____

_____

_____

_____

_____

_____

_____

_____

_____

_____

MINISTRY OPPORTUNITIES I AM PRAYING FOR

_____

_____

_____

_____

_____

_____

_____

_____

_____

_____

_____

_____

_____

_____

_____

_____

_____

HEALTH ISSUES I AM PRAYING FOR

_____

_____

_____

_____

_____

_____

_____

_____

_____

_____

_____

_____

_____

_____

_____

_____

NATIONS THAT NEED TO HEAR ABOUT JESUS

_____

_____

_____

_____

_____

_____

_____

_____

_____

_____

_____

_____

_____

_____

_____

_____

_____

_____

PRAYERS FOR MY COUNTRY

_____

_____

_____

_____

_____

_____

_____

_____

_____

_____

_____

_____

_____

_____

_____

_____

_____

WHERE HEALING IS NEEDED

_____

_____

_____

_____

_____

_____

_____

_____

_____

_____

_____

_____

_____

_____

_____

_____

_____

_____

_____

TROY SCHMIDT began writing animation in Los Angeles in 1985 (*Dennis the Menace, Heathcliff, Flintstone Kids*). In 1992, he moved to Orlando to write for *The Mickey Mouse Club* for three seasons. He adapted a Max Lucado children's book *Hermie* into a video, then created and wrote the future video installments and twenty Hermie books. Troy directed documentary footage in Israel for iLumina Gold, then returned in 2008 to host a documentary entitled "In His Shoes: The Life of Jesus" for GLO Bible software. Troy was also a producer for the GSN game show "The American Bible Challenge" starring Jeff Foxworthy and wrote the book and board game based on the show. He wrote two books for young men based on the Kendrick Brothers movies, "The War Room" and "Overcomer." Troy has served at Family Church in Central Florida since 1997 in a number of roles.

BOOKS
12 Truths & A Lie: Answers to Life's Biggest Questions (K-Love Books)
The Seven: Flood (Book 1) & Fire (Bood 2) (Brentwood)
How to Be a Superhero: Ten Superpowers God Gives You (Amazon)
The Whole Bible Story: Everything That Happens in the Bible (Bethany House)
Revealed (B&H Kids)
Fish Sandwiches: The Delight of Receiving God's Promises (NavPress)
The 100 Best Bible Verses for Mom (Amazon)
NIV Kid's Quiz Bible (Zondervan)
The 100 Best Bible Verses on Marriage, Family and Parenting (Amazon)
The 100 Best Bible Verses on Salvation (Amazon)
The 100 Most Confusing Verses in the Bible (Amazon)
Bible Trivia, Jokes & Fun Facts for Kids (Bethany House)
The Extreme Old/New Testament Bible Trivia Challenge (Broadstreet)
The Best 100 Bible Verses About Prayer (Bethany House)
The Best 100 Bible Verses About Heaven (Bethany House)
The 100 Most Encouraging Verses of the Bible (Bethany House)
This Means War: A Prayer Journal (B&H Kids)
The American Bible Challenge Daily Reader: Volume 1 (Thomas Nelson)
Chapter by Chapter: An Easy to Use Summary of the Entire Bible (Amazon)
Reason for Hope: Answers to Your Bible Questions (Amazon)
Reason for Hope: MORE Answers to Your Bible Questions (Amazon)
Reason for Hope: Answers to Your Questions about Heaven (Amazon)
40 Days: A Daily Devotion for Spiritual Renewal (Amazon)
Saved: Answers That Can Save Your Life (Amazon)
Release: Why God Wants You to Let Go (Amazon)
In His Shoes: The Life of Jesus (Amazon)
Laughing Matters (Lillenas Publishing)
Foundations: A Study of God (Amazon)
Living the Real Life: 12 Studies for Building Biblical Community (Amazon)

12 TRUTHS & A LIE:
ANSWERS TO LIFE'S BIGGEST QUESTIONS

Life is full of difficult questions and many of them often seem impossible to answer. In *12 Truths and a Lie: Answers to Life's Biggest Questions* , author and pastor J.D. Greear confidently tackles some of the most perplexing questions that Christians face. A collaboration with author and pastor J.D. Greear

FISH SANDWICHES:
THE DELIGHT OF RECEIVING GOD'S PROMISES

The Feeding of the 5,000 is the only miracle, besides the resurrection, mentioned in all four gospels. What was it about this miracle that every gospel writer felt they needed to mention? Fish Sandwiches (bread and fish) looks at 9 promises God communicated through that amazing miracle to apply to your life today and satisfy that hunger only Jesus can fulfill.

How to Be a Superhero: 10 Superpowers God Gives You to Make a Difference

God gives us the powers we need in the situations he determines. Walking through the Book of Judges, this book examines our God-given talents and personal uniqueness much like the superheroes of our day, both fictional and real. We can make a difference in a world desperately looking for heroes we can look up to. God can make you a superhero with the powers you already have!

THE 100 BEST BIBLE VERSES SERIES

The 100 verses that are highlighted include the well-known passages as well as hidden treasures. Each verse contains a brief devotional reading that will help you find comfort from the text, and in the process draw ever nearer to God. The book's length and focus make it perfect as a daily meditation or to read as a family. It also makes an ideal gift for those who love the Bible and seek the hope of God's promises.

REASON FOR HOPE:
ANSWERS TO YOUR BIBLE QUESTIONS

With over 50 answers to your Bible questions in every book, this book series answers some of the toughest questions people ask about God, their faith and the Bible.

IN HIS SHOES: THE LIFE OF JESUS

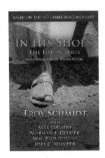

IN HIS SHOES: THE LIFE OF JESUS journeys to the all the places Jesus visited, from birth to death to resurrection and ascension. To help him along in his journey, Troy met up some of the greatest thinkers and writers from diverse perspectives to help him understand the experience (Max Lucado, Norman Geisler, William Paul Young, Joel Hunter and Avner Goren). The book includes a chapter-by-chapter Study Guide for Small Groups to use with the documentary which is available on the Glo Bible.

100 BEST BIBLE VERSES ON SALVATION

 This book examines the 100 best Bible verses from the New Testament that explain clearly what salvation through Jesus Christ is all about. Includes additional chapters from Troy's book "Saved" to help the reader understand even more clearly what it means to accept Christ. Perfect for new believers and seekers.

100 BEST BIBLE VERSES ON MARRIAGE, FAMILY & PARENTING

 A complete summary of all the best verses on the family, perfect for newlyweds, new parents or people who just want to strengthen their marriage. No other institution is under greater attack these days than the family. Discover God's best for all your relationships.

100 BEST BIBLE VERSES FOR MOM

 A book of biblical encouragement including verses to help every mom get through her day and show her that God appreciates her role in giving life to her family. The ideal gift to your love to your mom.

100 MOST CONFUSING VERSES IN THE BIBLE

 Easy to understand answers of the 100 most confusing, sometimes bizarre, passages we read in the Bible, explained with easy to understand answers.

CHAPTER BY CHAPTER: AN EASY-TO-USE SUMMARY OF THE ENTIRE BIBLE

The Bible is an intimidating book. It's easy to get lost in its pages. We all, sometimes, just need a little help to navigate through its pages. CHAPTER BY CHAPTER walks you through the Bible so that you understand all 929 chapters of the Old Testament and all 260 chapters of the New Testament. This book is not meant to replace your reading of God's word but it is useful as a reference guide to understand what you are reading or where to find passages and stories you know are in the Bible. It's time to begin your study of the entire Bible…chapter by chapter.

My number ONE seller on Amazon! Available on Kindle too.

The Whole Bible Story: Everything that Happens in the Bible

This young reader's edition of *The Whole Bible Story* will help you understand what the stories in the Bible are actually all about and how every single one of them fits together to tell one big story about God and his love for people--even you!

Along with the story of the Bible in words you can easily understand, in every chapter you will find great bonus material like exciting illustrations, fun facts and trivia about the Bible stories, simple lists of important characters and places, and easy-to-follow ways to apply the themes to your own life.

SAVED: ANSWERS THAT CAN SAVE YOUR LIFE

SAVED answers 25 questions that many ask before they find God—good questions, tough questions—that drown many in doubt and confusion before they find the answers. Questions such as: Do you have to know the Bible to be saved? Why was Jesus crucified? Is Christianity the only true faith? Don't we have to believe and do good works? Is the Trinity one God or three? How are those who never hear the Gospel saved? How am I saved?

RELEASE: WHY GOD WANTS YOU TO LET GO

Jesus focused on the concept of releasing. He told people to let go of things all the time. Why do we need to know that today? Our hands are so full that we can't receive God's blessing. Our grip is so tight that we can't grab on to what really matters. RELEASE explores this concept found throughout the Gospels – what was released and what the person received in return. From the characters in the parables to the real people in Jesus' life, we'll see that releasing our lives actually fills our lives.

40 DAYS: A DAILY DEVOTION FOR SPIRITUAL RENEWAL

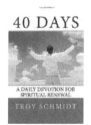

40 is a very significant number in the Bible, especially when it comes to 40 days. Some of most significant characters of the Old and New Testament had experiences that lasted 40 days—Noah, Moses, Joshua, David, Elijah, Ezekiel, Jonah, Jesus. What happened during that time and what did it take 40 days for them to experience? Renewal.

40 DAYS examines their life-changing encounters and draws from their lessons of transformation using 40 daily devotions you can use for your own renewal experience. It worked for them...why not you. After 40 days, you'll come back as good as new.

KID'S QUIZ BIBLE

 This full-feature Bible for ages 8-12 offers children a challenging experience as they delve into the Bible. Highlighting important facts and verses, the *NIV Kids' Quiz Bible* helps children engage with the text, while making it fun to learn all about God's Word! With answers to find in every book of the Bible, they won't want to stop reading. (Zondervan)

THIS MEANS WAR: A STRATEGIC PRAYER JOURNAL

 The teen years can be tough; don't try to make it through without one of your most powerful weapons—prayer. A companion book to the movie *War Room,* this new kind of journal will get you ready for a new kind of prayer life, one that's strong, growing, and reflects just how powerful prayer is. Each short chapter tackles one of the biggest questions teens have about prayer. Just-right journaling prompts will then get you thinking—and praying—and reinforce the real power of fighting battles on your knees.

THE AMERICAN BIBLE CHALLENGE DAILY READER

 In fall 2012, a new show premiered on the Game Show Network that quickly surprised Hollywood. Hosted by Jeff Foxworthy, *The American Bible Challenge* built up an audience of 2.3 million viewers in just nine weeks, making it the highest-rated show ever in GSN history. Now, the producer for the show, Troy Schmidt, with a foreword written by host Jeff Foxworthy, has released a daily reader based on *The American Bible Challenge* designed to take us deeper into the questions from the show and the life applications that they inspire.

PRAYING THROUGH THE BIBLE SERIES

PRAYING THROUGH THE BIBLE SERIES takes the reader through written prayers, with additional prompts to help you continue a focused time for prayer based on the passages. There is also space to record what God is saying to you during your time with Him. By the end, you will have prayed through God's word and gained a deeper appreciation for the Bible.

THE EXTREME OLD TESTAMENT / NEW TESTAMENT BIBLE TRIVIA CHALLENGE

Over 6,000 questions, written in the order as they appear in the Bible – from Genesis to Revelation. One question appears from EVERY chapter in the Bible. Great to use for a personal or group fun, for long car trips or morning devotions. Get to know the Bible in a fun and challenging way.

REVEALED

A young man's devotional based on the Kendrick Brother's movie "Overcomer." Written to help a young man discover God's intention and design in making each every one of us, "Revealed" dives deep into the best scriptures to allow the reader to his uniqueness and perfection in God's eyes. Written with Stephen and Alex Kendrick.

THE SEVEN:
FLOOD (Book 1) / FIRE (Book 2) / DARKNESS (Book 3)

A biblical fiction series following 7 young adults endowed with certain spiritual abilities as they travel through time to stop an enemy from disrupting biblical history. Their encounters put them right in the middle of the Bible's most incredible miracles.

THE GREATEST QUOTES JESUS EVER SAID
THE GREATEST QUESTIONS JESUS EVER ASKED
A 100 Day Devotional

  Begin every day with an inspirational thought and a life-changing challenge in these two daily devotionals that examine the best quotes and questions spoken by Jesus himself. (Amazon)

Made in the USA
Middletown, DE
25 March 2025